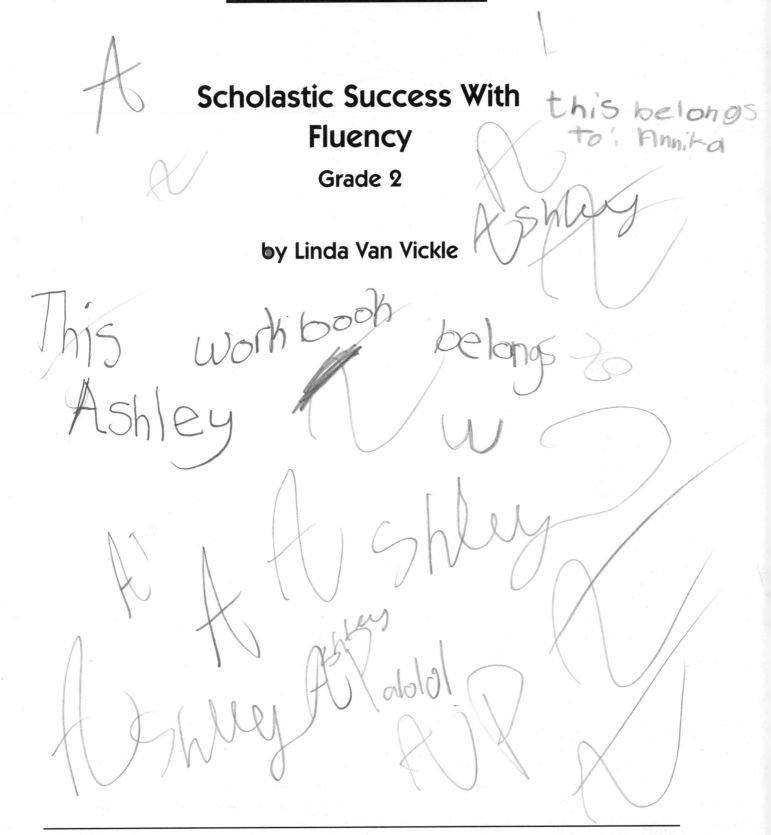

SCHOLASTIC

Scholastic Success With Fluency

Grade 2

by Linda Van Vickle

New York • Toronto • London • Auckland • Sydney
Mexico City • New Delhi • Hong Kong • Buenos Aires

Teaching *Resources*

Cover art by Amy Vangsgard
Cover design by Maria Lilja
Interior illustrations by Sherry Neidigh
Interior design by Quack & Company

ISBN 0-439-55386-5

Copyright © 2004 Scholastic, Inc.
All rights reserved. Printed in the U.S.A.

4 5 6 7 8 9 10   40   09 08

Introduction

Parents and teachers alike will find this book a valuable tool in helping students become fluent readers. Fluency is the ability to read smoothly and easily and is essential to reading comprehension. Prereading activities, which include building vocabulary and context, help students prepare for the readings. Decoding words ahead of time enables students to focus more attention on the actual meaning of the text. Activities are also designed to help students build their reading speed. By training their eyes to read more than one word at a time, students stay more focused and can better remember what they have read. This book also encourages students to read aloud with expression, which helps foster better comprehension. Students demonstrate their understanding of the readings in follow-up exercises and then extend this understanding through critical thinking questions. You will feel rewarded providing such a valuable resource for your students. Remember to praise them for their efforts and successes!

Table of Contents

Name Ashley

Benny's Flag

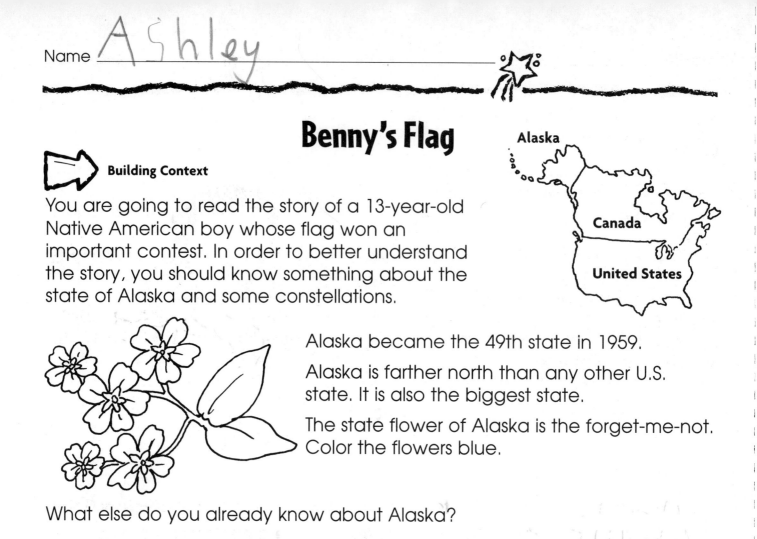

Alaska

Canada

United States

➡ **Building Context**

You are going to read the story of a 13-year-old Native American boy whose flag won an important contest. In order to better understand the story, you should know something about the state of Alaska and some constellations.

Alaska became the 49th state in 1959.

Alaska is farther north than any other U.S. state. It is also the biggest state.

The state flower of Alaska is the forget-me-not. Color the flowers blue.

What else do you already know about Alaska?

_____

_____

_____

Constellations are groups of stars. Long ago, people thought these groups of stars formed pictures in the sky. They named them after people, animals, and objects.

One constellation is called the Great Bear because people saw the shape of a bear when they looked at the group of stars. One group of stars in the Great Bear is called the Big Dipper. These stars look like a cup at the end of a long handle. The handle of the dipper forms the Great Bear's tail, and its cup forms part of the Bear's hindquarters.

Find the Big Dipper in the picture and outline it in red.

Name _____

➡ **Reading the Story**

In 1926 the governor of the territory of Alaska visited a post office building in Washington, D.C. There he saw flags from all the other territories and states, but none from Alaska. Since the United States had bought Alaska from Russia in 1867, Alaska had flown only the U.S. flag. The governor decided that Alaska needed its own flag.

A flag-design contest was held. All Alaskan school children in grades seven through twelve could enter. Children from all over the state sent in their designs for the flag. The judges had many designs to choose from, but after careful thought, they all agreed that Benny Benson's flag should win.

Thirteen-year-old Benny Benson was a student who grew up in Seward, Alaska. Benny's flag had a very simple design of a blue background with eight gold stars. Benny said that the blue background was for the Alaskan sky and the forget-me-not, an Alaskan flower. The North Star was for the future state of Alaska, the most northerly of the Union. The dipper was for the Great Bear, showing strength.

Benny won $1,000 and a gold watch for his winning flag. His flag helped tell the people in Alaska to work toward becoming a state. In 1959, when Alaska became a state, Benny's flag was made the state flag.

Thinking About What You Read

1. Benny's flag had a very simple design: eight gold stars on a blue background. Color the flag using the colors Benny chose.

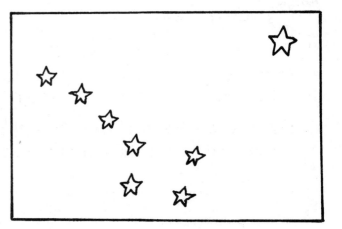

Benny kept his flag very simple because he used symbols. A symbol is something that makes people think of something else. For example a heart is a symbol for love. Think about what Benny's symbols told about Alaska.

2. Why did Benny choose a blue background?

_____

_____

3. Why did Benny choose the North Star to stand for Alaska?

_____

_____

4. The Big Dipper is part of the constellation called the Great Bear. Why is a bear a good symbol for Alaska?

_____

_____

5. Benny's design was simple, but everything about it stood for something about Alaska. On another sheet of paper, design a flag for your school. Try to use just a few symbols that show what is most important about your school.

Animal-Friendly Zoo

Building Context

You can better understand what you read if you think about the subject before you begin. Here are some questions to think about before you read the story of Carl Hagenbeck and his famous zoo in Germany.

1. A *menagerie* is a collection of wild animals. If you could have a menagerie or a fishing business, which would you want? Why?

_____

_____

_____

2. How do you think people who work with animals should treat them?

_____

_____

_____

3. Until 1907 all the animals in zoos were locked up in steel cages. How are most zoos different today?

_____

_____

_____

4. If you could design your own zoo, what would it have in it? What would it look like?

_____

_____

_____

Building Reading Speed

By practicing some of the words you will read in a story, you can improve your reading speed.

Here are some of the words you will find in the story of Carl Hagenbeck's zoo. Practice reading the words on the chart three times, reading a little faster each time.

fisherman	washtub	steel bars	circuses	popular	visitors
menagerie	respect	business	sailors	interest	zoos
importantly	display	company	pastures	habitat	seals
fortunately	moats	borrowed	trenches	gently	dream

Use a word from the chart to answer each question.

1. What animals that live near water might be caught in fishermen's nets?

s __ __ __ __

2. What word describes how zoos and circuses should treat their animals?

g __ __ __ __ __

3. What word means the natural home of an animal?

h __ __ __ __ __ __

4. What words name ways to separate people from the animals they are watching?

s __ __ __ __ __   b __ __ __ __, m __ __ __ __, and

t __ __ __ __ __ __ __

Scholastic Teaching Resources

➡ **Reading the Story**

If you visited a U.S. zoo in the early 1900s, you would have seen animals locked up in rows of steel cages. The first zoos did little more than put animals in cages for people to see. Fortunately for zoo visitors and for the animals, Carl Hagenbeck had a better idea.

Hagenbeck's interest in animals began when he was a small boy. His father, who sold fish, also cared for the seals caught in his fishermen's nets. He kept the seals in a washtub. Over the years, he bought other animals from sailors and soon had a small menagerie. When Carl became a young man, his father gave him a choice: he could take over the fishing business, or he could take over the animals. Carl Hagenbeck chose the animals.

Soon Hagenbeck turned his father's small menagerie into the world's largest company dealing in animals. He supplied animals to zoos and circuses all over the world. Hagenbeck began to see animals as more than a business. Working closely with animals, he came to respect and love them. He believed animals could be trained gently. His "Tamed Animal Performances" became very popular all over the world.

Hagenbeck dreamed of a "zoo of the future," a zoo without bars. In 1907 Hagenbeck's dream became real when he opened his zoo outside the city of Hamburg, Germany. Instead of steel bars, trenches and moats separated the people from the animals. Hagenbeck turned pastures and fields into natural habitats for his animals. Today, Hagenbeck's zoo is still run by his family. More importantly, zoos all over the world have borrowed Hagenbeck's ideas. They show animals in natural habitats and treat animals with respect.

➡ **Reading With Expression**

Imagine that you were invited to the grand opening of Carl Hagenbeck's zoo. You have been asked to read a poem for this special event. Since it would be an exciting, happy event, show those feelings when you read. The writer of this poem uses an exclamation point (!) to show places in the poem where your voice should sound most excited. Find these three places in the poem and circle them.

Come to the Zoo

Come along, come along,
On a trip to the zoo!
We'll see a swinging chimpanzee
And a kangaroo (or two!)
And maybe a zebra, taking a drink,
And a roaring lion,
And, what do you think?
A tall giraffe, plucking leaves from a tree—
Come along to the zoo
And see them with me!

     Helen H. Moore

Why do you think this poem would be a good choice for the zoo opening?

_____

_____

Now practice reading the poem aloud a few times. Then read it for your classmates just as you would read it for Carl Hagenbeck's celebration.

Think about how your voice sounds when you ask a question like "Can I go outside?" Find the place in the poem where the author wants your voice to sound like you are asking a question. Underline that line.

The author also wants you to pause so you do not read too fast. She uses commas (,) to shows these places. Circle the commas so you remember to pause.

How NOT to Catch a Cold

Building Context

1. Have you ever had a bad cold? Tell what is was like and how you felt.

   It felt the worst thing in my life

2. What do you do to get over a cold? What helps you feel a little better when you are sick?

   I drink a little water ev.

3. What do you think causes a cold?

4. Have you heard people say, "Try not to catch a cold"? What do you do to keep from catching a cold when a lot of people around you are sick?

Building Vocabulary

You are going to read an article that tells some steps you can take so you do not catch a cold. Before you begin, practice reading some of the words that are used in the article. If you know these words and their meanings, you will be able to better understand the article. Read through the words in the chart three times, trying to read a little faster each time.

| diseases | vaccine | habit | infecting | treatment |
| virus | avoid | inhale | healthy | immune system |

To make sure you know the meanings of all these words, match each word with its definition. Use a dictionary to help you.

a. avoid ___ to breathe in

b. healthy ___ making sick

c. diseases ___ stay away from

d. habits ___ not sick or injured

e. immune system ___ microscopic organism that causes illness

f. infecting ___ a shot given to prevent illness or disease

g. inhale ___ conditions that leave the body sick or weak

h. treatment ___ steps to cure an illness

i. vaccine ___ actions done regularly

j. virus ___ system in the body that fights off disease

Scholastic Teaching Resources

Reading the Article

Did you know that each child in school catches six to ten colds every year? Think about it: all that sneezing, a sore throat, and a runny nose—ten times a year! Although doctors have found cures for many diseases, there is still no cure for the cold. A virus causes a cold. There are too many different kinds of viruses for one treatment, like a vaccine, to cure them all. Although there is no cure, there are some steps you can take to avoid getting a cold.

First, you can avoid catching a cold by practicing healthy habits. If you are healthy, your body's immune system has a better chance to fight off the viruses that cause colds. Begin by eating healthy foods. Eat lots of fruits and vegetables and drink milk and juice. Other healthy habits include getting plenty of sleep at night and lots of exercise.

Next, you should try to avoid contact with the viruses that cause colds. If you can, stay away from large crowds. When people cough and sneeze, the cold virus goes into the air. If you inhale the virus, you can catch a cold. Do not share a drinking cup, fork, or spoon with someone else because that, too, could spread the virus. Washing your hands is one of the best ways not to catch a cold. The cold virus may be on things like doorknobs, telephones, and money. Shaking another person's hand could even spread the virus. By washing your hands, you can stop the virus from infecting you.

Until doctors find a way to stop the over 200 viruses that cause colds, follow the steps listed above. You might avoid catching a cold.

Name _____

Thinking About What You Read

This article told you ways to avoid catching a cold. Some of it you may have known before you began reading, and some of it may have been new to you. To see what you remember, mark the sentences *T* for true or *F* for false.

1. ____ Colds can be cured with a vaccine.

2. ____ Your digestive system fights off colds.

3. ____ One of the best ways to avoid colds is washing your hands.

4. ____ You can avoid colds by avoiding large crowds.

5. ____ Sharing drinking cups will not spread colds.

6. ____ You can catch a cold from touching a doorknob.

Did thinking about the subject of the article before you read it help you remember more of the facts? Why or why not?

_____

_____

_____

List three words you learned from the article.

_____

_____

List two facts you did not know before you read the article.

_____

_____

Scholastic Teaching Resources

Name _____

Getting to Know Sue

Building Context

1. You are going to be reading about a dinosaur. Write down some things that you know about dinosaurs.

   They have sharp teeth.

   They Rore

2. You are going to be reading about one type of dinosaur called *Tyrannosaurus rex* or *T. rex* for short. What do you know about this dinosaur?

   It stomps it's feet.

Which picture do you think is a *T. rex*? Circle it.

What do you think a *T. rex* would try to do if it met up with any of those other dinosaurs?

a. run away from them

b. try to eat them

c. join them in eating a lunch of grass and leaves

3. Since the last dinosaur died millions of years ago, we know about dinosaurs only through their fossils—their remains left in rock. Here are the events that occurred to form dinosaur fossils. Put them in the order that you think they happened.

   ____ The dinosaur died and sank into mud and sand.

   ____ These minerals formed a fossil.

   ____ The dinosaur began to decay and was buried under mud and sand.

   ____ The dinosaur's bones were replaced with minerals.

By Ashley

By: Ashley

➡️ **Building Vocabulary**

Before you begin reading about the dinosaur, learn the meanings of some of the words you will find. Knowing these words will help you read faster and will help you better understand what you read.

Here are some words used to describe the dinosaur you will read about. Practice reading the words in the chart three times. See if you can read them a little faster each time.

bones	skeleton	brain	ribs	claws	teeth	skull	tail

When you read about the dinosaur, you will also come across a lot of action words that end in -ed. Practice reading these words. See if you can read them a little faster each time.

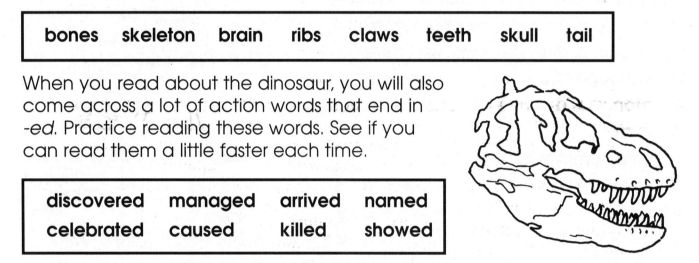

discovered	managed	arrived	named
celebrated	caused	killed	showed

Read the story. Then match the names of the people, animals, and places below with what each one is.

____ *Tyrannosaurus rex*

____ *T. rex*

____ Sue Hendrickson

____ Sue

____ Gypsy

____ Black Hills, South Dakota

____ Field Museum in Chicago

a. Sue Hendrickson's dog

b. a natural science center in Illinois

c. a mountainous desert area

d. a woman who collects fossils

e. a very big meat-eating dinosaur

f. name given to a *T. rex* skeleton

g. *Tyrannosaurus rex's* nickname

Scholastic Teaching Resources

Name _____

Reading the Story

Poor Sue must have had a rough life. Its ribs had been broken. Its skull showed damage from disease. It was not easy being a fierce *Tyrannosaurus rex*. Still, Sue managed to live a long life and to grow quite large before it died in a fast-moving river. How do we know so much about Sue, a dinosaur that died millions of years ago? Sue's nearly complete skeleton was discovered, and the bones tell its story.

In the summer of 1990, Sue Hendrickson was hunting for fossils in the Black Hills of South Dakota with her dog, Gypsy. While climbing a cliff, she saw some really big bones in the rocks. She thought she had found a *T. rex*. When the rest of her fossil-hunting team arrived, they celebrated Sue's discovery and named the skeleton Sue in her honor. The Field Museum in Chicago bought the *T. rex* for more than eight million dollars, the most ever paid for a fossil. Today, Sue stands in the museum for visitors to admire and for scientists to study.

From the skeleton, scientists know that Sue was 42 feet long and stood 13 feet high at its hips. When it was alive, Sue weighed seven tons. Its skull alone weighed 600 pounds. In the skull are 58 large teeth. Some are a foot long, big enough to crush bones. The skull shows that Sue had a very good sense of smell. Sue's strong legs show that Sue could move very fast. From Sue's skeleton and sharp claws, scientists think that the *T. rex* was a fierce and powerful hunter. Sue could have killed and eaten any other dinosaur of the time. Some of Sue's own injuries were most likely caused by fights with another *T. rex*.

Sue may have lived millions of years ago, but through its bones, scientists are still learning a lot about it.

Scholastic Teaching Resources

➡️ **Thinking About What You Read**

1. Why do scientists think the *T. rex* Sue was in a lot of fights?

_____

_____

2. Why do scientists think Sue was a "fierce and powerful hunter" that probably ate other dinosaurs?

_____

_____

3. Why did the fossil hunting team name the *T. rex* skeleton "Sue"?

_____

_____

_____

4. Why do you think the Field Museum paid so much money for Sue?

_____

_____

5. Sue's skeleton can tell scientists a lot of information, but what do you think scientists cannot learn from just bones?

_____

_____

Scholastic Teaching Resources

Otzi's Outfit

> **Building Context**

Food can be kept in a freezer for a long time. When it is taken out and thawed, the food is still fresh. The cold freezer preserves the food. That means it keeps the food from rotting and going bad.

You are going to read the story of a man who died thousands of years ago. Because he was covered with ice and snow, he froze, and his body and all of his clothes were preserved. Scientists have been able to study this man and learn much about how people lived long ago.

Thousands of years ago, people had to make their clothes out of materials they found in nature. Think about what materials they might have used to make clothes. List your ideas below.

leaves
coton
w

Now imagine that a person had to make clothes to wear when walking over a very cold mountain using only materials from your list. Draw a picture of how you think that person would dress.

Building Vocabulary

Here are some of the words you will find in the story about the Ice Man.
Practice reading the list three times, trying to read a little faster each time.

mountains	window	soles
preserved	leggings	sewn
Germany	material	icy
shoulders	ancient	Alps
cloak	tendons	Italy
waterproof	glacier	valley
attached	woven	outfit
understanding	leather	hikers

Use the words from the chart to complete the following sentences. There
are letter clues to help you.

1. Two European countries are __ __ __ m __ __ __ and
   __ t __ __ __. The __ __ p __ is a mountain range in Europe.

2. __ __ k __ __ __ are people who go on long walks.

3. A __ __ a __ __ __ __ r is a large mass of moving ice found on
   mountains.

4. S __ __ __ s are the bottoms of shoes.

5. Something that is very old is said to be __ n __ __ __ __ t.

6. In animals, the tissues that hold the muscles to the bones are called
   __ __ n d __ __ __.

Building Reading Speed

When you slowly read one word at a time, you may find it hard to stay interested in what you are reading. Reading faster may help you understand and remember more of what you read. You can become a faster reader by practicing reading more than one word at a time. You do this by training your eyes to see words in groups rather than as single words. Practice reading part of "Otzi's Outfit" in word groups.

People who lived
5,000 years ago
had to keep warm
as they traveled
across cold mountains.
There were no stores
where they could buy
warm clothes and boots.
They had to make
their clothes
out of the materials
around them.
What do you think
they wore?
   Today we know
the answer
to that question
because of Otzi,
the Ice Man.
Over 5,000 years ago,
the Ice Man died
while trying
to cross the Alps.
His body lay frozen

in an icy glacier
until 1991.
Two hikers found him
in the Otz Valley
on the border
of Italy and Austria.
This is why
he is called "Otzi."
The ice had not only
preserved Otzi's body
but also his clothes.

Now read this part of "Otzi's Outfit" again. This time have someone time you. Record your time here. _____

Now practice reading the rest of "Otzi's Outfit" three times. Have someone time you. Record your times in the chart below. Try to read a little faster each time.

To keep his head warm,
Otzi wore a fur
bowl-shaped cap
tied to his head
with leather straps.
His leather shirt
was shaped
like a cape and
sewn together
with animal tendons.
        On his legs,
Otzi wore two separate
leather "leggings."
The tops were tied
with leather strips
to his belt.
The bottom part
of each legging
had a long flap
that could be tucked
into the shoe.
Otzi's shoes
had soles made
of brown bear skin.
The soles were attached
to "nets"
made of deerskin
that wrapped
over the feet.

In the winter,
Otzi may have
stuffed dry grass
into the netting
for extra warmth.
        Over this entire outfit,
Otzi wore
a sleeveless cloak
of woven grass.
Otzi pulled
this cloak over
his head and shoulders,
and it hung
to his knees.
Otzi may have
covered the coat
in animal fat
to make it waterproof.
        While it is sad
that Otzi
did not survive
his journey
over the mountains,
he has given us
a window
into the past
and a greater understanding
of how ancient people lived.

#1 _____	#2 _____	#3 _____

Scholastic Teaching Resources

Name _____

➡ **Reading the Story**

People who lived 5,000 years ago had to keep warm as they traveled across cold mountains. There were no stores where they could buy warm clothes and boots. They had to make their clothes out of the materials around them. What do you think they wore?

Today we know the answer to that question because of Otzi, the Ice Man. Over 5,000 years ago, the Ice Man died while trying to cross the Alps. His body lay frozen in an icy glacier until 1991. Two hikers found him in the Otz Valley on the border of Italy and Austria. This is why he is called "Otzi." The ice had not only preserved Otzi's body but also his clothes.

To keep his head warm, Otzi wore a fur bowl-shaped cap tied to his head with leather straps. His leather shirt was shaped like a cape and sewn together with animal tendons.

On his legs, Otzi wore two separate leather "leggings." The tops were tied with leather strips to his belt. The bottom part of each legging had a long flap that could be tucked into the shoe. Otzi's shoes had soles made of brown bear skin. The soles were attached to "nets" made of deerskin that wrapped over the feet. In the winter, Otzi may have stuffed dry grass into the netting for extra warmth.

Over this entire outfit, Otzi wore a sleeveless cloak of woven grass. Otzi pulled this cloak over his head and shoulders, and it hung to his knees. Otzi may have covered the coat in animal fat to make it waterproof.

While it is sad that Otzi did not survive his journey over the mountains, he has given us a window into the past and a greater understanding of how ancient people lived.

Name _____

The Mouse and the Lion
(A Fable by Aesop)

 **Building Context**

Fables are short stories that are told to teach lessons about life. Many of the fables we still tell today are said to come from Aesop (e-sop), a man who may have lived in Greece during the 6th century B.C. The characters in Aesop's fables are often talking animals. Aesop's fables are fun to read and to hear because of these animals and because they teach important lessons.

1. One of Aesop's most popular fables tells the story of a mouse and a lion. Think about how very different these two animals are. Show these differences by listing words that describe each animal.

Lion	Mouse
_____	_____
_____	_____
_____	_____

2. What do you think a lion would do with a mouse if it caught one?

_____

_____

3. Could a mouse ever help a lion? Explain how or why not.

_____

_____

_____

_____

Name _____

➤ Reading the Story

One day, a great lion was asleep under a tree.
A little mouse began playing on the lion. The mouse
ran over the lion's back and across his paws and soon
woke him up. The angry lion caught the mouse under
his huge paw and growled, "You have disturbed my
nap, and for that I am going to eat you!"

Just as the lion opened his big jaws to swallow the
mouse, the tiny creature cried, "Please don't eat me, King Lion. I am sorry
for waking you up. Forgive me, and I promise I will help you some day."

The lion began to laugh. "How could a little mouse like you help a
mighty lion like me?" he asked. "The idea is so funny. I will let you go this
time because you have made me laugh." The lion lifted his paw, and the
mouse ran away.

"Thank you! Thank you!" the mouse called. "I will never forget my
promise."

Days later, the lion was caught in a trap by some hunters who tied him to
a tree with a heavy rope. Then the hunters went off to get their wagon to
carry the lion off to the king's zoo. The lion roared and pulled, but he could
not break free from the heavy rope that held him.

The little mouse heard all the noise and came to see what had
happened. When he saw the lion tied to the tree, he ran up to him and
began to chew on the heavy ropes. In a short while, he chewed through the
rope, and the lion was free.

The lion turned to the mouse and said,
"Thank you, my little friend. I am sorry that
I laughed at you."

As the lion bounded off into the forest,
the little mouse called out to him, "Always
remember that even a little friend may
someday be a great friend!"

Reading With Expression

When the two characters in "The Mouse and the Lion" speak, they are expressing different feelings. Thinking about these feeling as you read the words to yourself or showing these emotions in your voice when you read aloud makes the story better.

Describe the feelings of the mouse and lion by answering the questions. Then read their words in a way that shows those feelings.

1. **How was the lion feeling after the mouse woke him up?**

_____

Read: "You have disturbed my nap, and for that I am going to eat you!"

2. **How was the mouse feeling when he thought the lion was going to eat him?**

_____

Read: "Please don't eat me, King Lion. I am sorry for waking you up. Forgive me, and I promise I will help you some day."

3. **How did the lion feel when the mouse first said that he would help the lion some day?**

_____

Read: "How could a little mouse like you help a mighty lion like me? The idea is so funny. I will let you go this time because you have made me laugh."

4. How did the mouse feel when he knew the lion was going to let him go and not eat him?

_____

Read: "Thank you! Thank you! I will never forget my promise."

5. How did the lion feel when he realized that a little mouse really could help a mighty lion?

_____

Read: "Thank you, my little friend. I am sorry that I laughed at you."

6. The little mouse gets the last words in this story. He reminds the lion of an important lesson. What was he feeling as he spoke these words?

_____

Read: "Always remember that even a little friend may someday be a great friend!"

After you have thought about how the animals say their words and the feelings their words show, read the lines out loud. See if your classmates can guess the feelings you are trying to show with just the sound of your voice.

Then read the whole fable "The Mouse and the Lion" again. This time as you read, think about how the characters are feeling as they speak.

Name _____

The Boy Who Cried "Wolf"
(A Fable by Aesop)

Reading With Expression

Writers use punctuation marks so readers know how the characters in a story are speaking. If the characters are simply making a statement, the writer will use a comma (**,**) or a period (**.**).

> **"It is raining," said Tom.**
>
> **Tom said, "It is raining."**

The writer shows that a character is asking a question by using a question mark (**?**).

> **"Did you bring an umbrella?" asked Mary.**

If a character is yelling or showing strong feelings, the writer will use an exclamation point (**!**).

> **"Bring a bucket quick! The roof is leaking!" cried Tom.**

Here are some of the characters' lines that you will read in the fable "The Boy Who Cried 'Wolf.'" Decide how the speakers are saying these lines and add the correct punctuation.

"Wolf Wolf Help "

"Where is the wolf "

"I played a trick on you "

"Why didn't you help me when I called for you "

"Once you tell a lie, no one will believe you can tell the truth"

Name _____

➡ **Reading the Story**

Once there lived a young boy whose job was to watch sheep. Every day he would lead his sheep to the fields of green grass outside his village. The boy would sit in the shade all day watching his sheep eat grass. He often grew very bored with his job. He wanted some excitement in his long day.

One day he decided to have some fun by playing a trick. After he led his sheep to the pasture, he called out loudly, "Wolf! Wolf! Help!" When the people in the village heard his cry, they came running to help the boy and to save his sheep. But when they arrived at the field, there was no wolf.

"Where is the wolf?" they asked. "We left our work to help you."

The boy began to laugh. "There is no wolf," he said. "I played a trick on you." The people shook their heads. They did not think the trick was very funny. Then they went back to the village.

A few days later, the young boy decided to play his trick again. He waited until it was hot in the afternoon and then called, "Wolf! Wolf! Help!"

Again, the people in the village left their jobs and ran to help the young boy. They reached the field, hot and out of breath. "Where is the wolf?" they asked.

"I tricked you again!" the young boy laughed.

This time the village people were angry. "You should not call for help if you do not need help," they said as they began the walk back to the village.

The next day while the boy was resting in the shade and watching his sheep, a wolf appeared. It began chasing the sheep. The young boy was very afraid. He knew that he could not protect his sheep from the wolf. "Wolf! Wolf! Help!" he cried.

But when the people in the village heard his call, they said, "That boy is trying to trick us again." The people went back to their work and did not go to help the boy. The hungry wolf ate all of his sheep.

The boy returned to the village and told everyone what happened. "Why didn't you help me when I called for you?" he asked.

"Once you tell a lie," the people said, "no one will believe you can tell the truth."

Name _____

Thinking About What You Read

1. The boy in the story had to sit out in the fields all day doing nothing but watching his sheep. He was bored. Was this a good reason to play a trick on the people in his village? Why or why not?

_____

_____

_____

2. If the boy had played the trick only one time, do you think the people would have come to help him when the wolf really did come? Why or why not?

_____

_____

_____

3. Do you think the people of the village will ever believe the boy can tell the truth? Why or why not?

_____

_____

_____

4. From this story has come the expression "Don't cry 'wolf'." What does it mean if someone tells you "Don't cry 'wolf'"?

_____

_____

_____

Scholastic Teaching Resources

The Snowflake Man

Building Context

Scientists study a field of science until they become experts. That means they know a lot about the subject. There are many fields of science and many kinds of scientists. Some study medicine, some study the ocean, some study plants, and some study animals.

You are going to read about scientists who study the weather. To better understand why weather changes, they study the clouds and how the winds blow around the earth. This kind of scientist is called a **meteorologist**, and the study of weather is called **meteorology**.

What do you think it takes to make a good scientist? Place checks by the words that you think describe a good scientist.

____ **someone who has gone to college and studied**
____ **someone who has done a lot of research**
____ **someone who has lots of money**
____ **someone who loves science**
____ **someone whom everybody likes**
____ **someone who writes a lot of books and articles**
____ **someone who makes new discoveries in science**
____ **someone who uses a lot of equipment to study a science**

Now look at what you have checked. Which of those do you think is the most important characteristic for a scientist to have?

_____

_____

Building Vocabulary

Have you ever heard someone say, "No two snowflakes are alike"? Well, it is true. The first person who found that out had to look at a lot of snowflakes. That person was Wilson Bentley. He looked at so many snowflakes and took so many pictures of them that he became known as the "Snowflake Man."

Scholastic Teaching Resources

Name Ashley Pablo

Before you begin reading about Wilson Bentley, you should practice reading some of the words you will find in his story. Read over the list of words three times. Then make sure you know the meanings of those words by completing the puzzle. Use a dictionary to help you.

Vermont	published	strange	photographs
pioneer	experimented	dew	microscope
scientist	meteorological	camera	discovered

Across

2. odd, unusual

6. the first one to do something

10. having to do with the study of weather

11. to have printed for everyone to read

12. water drops that form on the grass at night

Down

1. used for taking pictures

3. pictures taken with a camera

4. to have found something for the first time

5. one who has great knowledge of science

7. a U.S. state

8. tested to find out information

9. used to see very tiny objects

Scholastic Teaching Resources

➡️ **Reading the Story**

When he was a young boy in Vermont, Wilson Bentley enjoyed looking at things under the microscope his mother had given him. Most of all, he loved to look at snowflakes. He spent hours looking at them. He tried to draw them, but his drawings were never as beautiful as what he saw in his microscope.

One day he read about a special camera. It could take pictures through a microscope. He begged his parents to get him this camera. His father thought getting a camera to take pictures of snowflakes was silly. But Bentley's mother understood, and together they talked his father into getting the camera. For a year Bentley worked with the camera and his microscope. Finally, during a snowstorm on January 15, 1885, he took the first microscopic picture of a snowflake. For the rest of his life, Bentley studied and photographed snowflakes. He also studied and experimented with raindrops and dew. He took over 5,000 photographs and wrote many scientific articles.

Bentley's neighbors in the small Vermont town never did understand his love of snowflakes. They thought he was a nice man but very strange. For many years, Bentley did not tell the world of his discoveries. He did not think scientists would listen to him because he did not go to college. A scientist soon learned of Bentley's work and convinced him that his careful weather studies and beautiful snowflake photographs were important. In 1924 the American Meteorological Society awarded Bentley its first research grant ever, for all his years of work. Seven years later, nearly 2,500 of his photographs were published in a book, *Snow Crystals*. Today, scientists know that Bentley was a pioneer in the study of weather. For Bentley, the greatest reward for his work was sharing the beauty he discovered in the snowflakes he saw under his microscope.

Thinking About What You Read

1. How do you know that Wilson Bentley really loved to study snowflakes?

   _____

   _____

   _____

2. Look back through the story. How many times are the words *beautiful* and *beauty* used? _____ times

3. Bentley was a scientist, so he learned many facts about snow, but what do you think he liked best about it?

   _____

   _____

4. For most of his life, Bentley studied without most people's help and support. In fact, most people did not even think he should study snow and weather. Who were some of these people?

   _____

   _____

5. Place a check by what you most admire about Bentley.

   _____ He was the first to take a picture of a snowflake.

   _____ He was awarded a grant by the American Meteorological Society.

   _____ He did what he loved no matter what others thought.

   _____ He published articles and a book.

   Explain why that was your choice.

   _____

   _____

   _____

Name _____

Reading With Expression

Imagine that you have been invited to help honor Wilson Bentley when he gets his grant from the American Meteorological Society. You have been asked to read one of these two poems.

Snow Stars

Delicate
And feathery,
Crystal clear
And white,
Six-point stars
Come tumbling,
Softly
In the night.

Regina Sauro

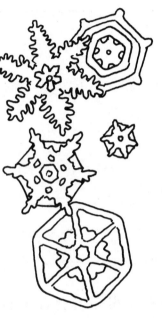

White Snow

The snow is white and clean.

It makes a lovely scene.

It covers cars, and trees, and streets,

and makes the world go "hush."

It looks so very pretty—

until it turns to slush!

Helen H. Moore

1. Which of the poems do you think should be read in a softer voice? Why?

_____

_____

2. Which poem has more words that rhyme? _____

3. Which of the two poems do you think Bentley would like most of all? Why? _____

_____

Practice reading the poem you have chosen. Be sure to pay attention to the commas (,) and periods (.) at the ends of the lines. These are places the poet wants you to pause when you are reading. Also, remember you are reading the poem for someone who loves the beauty of snow. Try to show a love and enjoyment of snow in your voice as you read the poem aloud.

Master of Disguise

 **Building Vocabulary**

You are going to read about an insect that is very good at hiding: the walkingstick.

Before reading about this insect, practice reading some of the words you will find in the story that follows.

motionless	sway	spiders	rodents
disturbed	twig	predator	reptiles
underbrush	fails	disguise	slender
deliberately	birds	branches	insect

Now see if you understand the meanings of these words by using them to answer the following questions. Use a dictionary to help you.

1. **What word describes standing very still?**

m __ __ __ __ __ __ __ __ __

2. **What word means to change the way something looks?**

d __ __ __ __ __ __ __

3. **What word means doing something on purpose?**

__ __ __ __ __ b __ __ __ __ __ __ __

4. *Predators* **are insects and animals that eat other insects and animals. What four words name predators that might eat a walkingstick?**

b __ __ __ __ , s __ __ __ __ __ __ , d __ __ __ __ __ __ ,

and __ __ P __ __ __ __ __ __

5. **What word is used to describe a small stick?** __ w __ __

6. **What word means thin or skinny?** __ l __ __ __ __ __

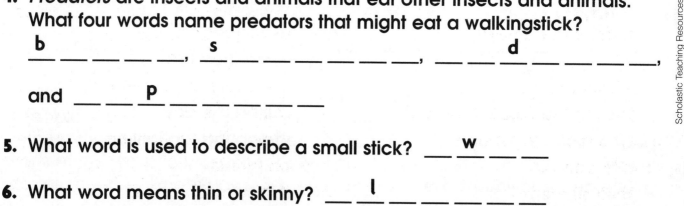

Scholastic Teaching Resources

Building Speed

When you slowly read one word at a time, you may find it hard to stay interested in what you are reading. Reading faster may help you understand and remember more of what you read.

Practicing reading new words and knowing their meanings can help you be a faster reader. You can also become a faster reader by practicing reading more than one word at a time. You do this by training your eyes to see words in groups rather than as single words.

Practice doing this as you read about the walkingstick. Try to read each line of the story at once rather than reading each individual word.

**The longest insect
in the United States
is a walkingstick,
which can reach
a length of five inches.
It is big,
but the walkingstick
is one of
the hardest insects
to find.
While many insects
use their color and shape
to hide from hungry predators,
the walkingstick
is a true
master of disguise.**

**Walkingsticks
live on the plants they eat
and look very much
like part of
their dinner.**

**As its name suggests,
the walkingstick
has a long, slender body
that is the color and shape
of a stick or twig.
Walkingsticks
usually eat at night
when they are
less likely to be seen.
During the day
they hang motionless
on plants.
If they must move,**

walkingsticks sway slowly
from side to side,
so they look like
tiny branches
moving in the wind.
Walkingsticks
even begin
their lives in disguise.
The tiny eggs
they hatch from
look like seeds.

Sometimes even
the best disguises
do not work.
Hungry birds, rodents,
reptiles, and spiders
are always on the lookout
for a tasty walkingstick.
If a walkingstick
is disturbed,
it will first fall
to the ground
and play dead.

Some walkingsticks
are able to give off
a bad smell,
which will chase off
some predators.
But if all else fails,
the walkingstick
has one more trick.
If a hungry predator
tries to carry it off,
the walkingstick
will deliberately
lose its own leg.
The predator is left
with a leg
while the walkingstick
falls to the ground
and blends in
with the underbrush.
When it is safe,
the walkingstick
slowly walks away,
and in no time
grows a new leg!

Scholastic Teaching Resources

➡️ **Thinking About What You Read**

1. Did trying to read the words in groups help you read faster? Tell why or why not.

_____

_____

2. What are some words you understand better now after reading the story?

_____

_____

3. What do you most remember about the walkingstick after reading the story?

_____

_____

_____

4. What was something you learned about the walkingstick that you did not know before?

_____

_____

Now read the story again. This time the story looks like it would in a book. See if you can still read groups of words at a time rather than one word at a time.

Reading the Story

The longest insect in the United States is a walkingstick, which can reach a length of five inches. It is big, but the walkingstick is one of the hardest insects to find. While many insects use their color and shape to hide from hungry predators, the walkingstick is a true master of disguise.

Walkingsticks live on the plants they eat and look very much like part of their dinner. As its name suggests, the walkingstick has a long, slender body that is the color and shape of a stick or twig. Walkingsticks usually eat at night when they are less likely to be seen. During the day they hang motionless on plants. If they must move, walkingsticks sway slowly from side to side, so they look like tiny branches moving in the wind. Walkingsticks even begin their lives in disguise. The tiny eggs they hatch from look like seeds.

Sometimes even the best disguises do not work. Hungry birds, rodents, reptiles, and spiders are always on the lookout for a tasty walkingstick. If a walkingstick is disturbed, it will first fall to the ground and play dead. Some walkingsticks are able to give off a bad smell, which will chase off some predators. But if all else fails, the walkingstick has one more trick. If a hungry predator tries to carry it off, the walkingstick will deliberately lose its own leg. The predator is left with a leg while the walkingstick falls to the ground and blends in with the underbrush. When it is safe, the walkingstick slowly walks away, and in no time grows a new leg!

Scholastic Teaching Resources

→ **Thinking About What You Read**

Practice reading the poem until you know the words and can say the whole poem without looking at the page.

1. *Queer* means very strange or odd. Why does the poet choose that word to describe the stick she found?

   _____

   _____

   _____

   _____

"A Queer Twig"

Out in the woods I found today
   A queer thing, without doubt—
A wee twig that did not stay still,
   But tried to walk about.

I thought this funny twig had planned
   To play a funny trick,
Until I learned it was a bug
   Known as the "walkingstick."

Alice Crowell Hoffman

2. *Wee* means very small or tiny. Is a walkingstick always very small?

   _____

   _____

3. Someone who had never heard of a walkingstick would have a hard time understanding this poem. If a friend read this poem and did not understand it, how would you explain it to him or her?

   _____

   _____

   _____

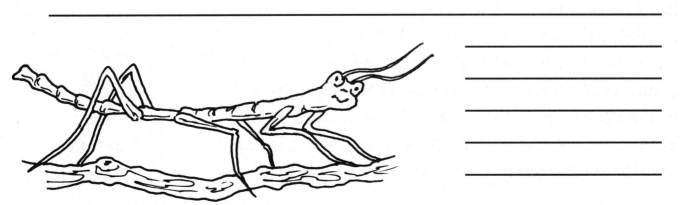

   _____

   _____

   _____

   _____

   _____

   _____

Name _____

Tricky Tenali Raman
(Folktale From India)

▶ **Building Vocabulary**

People all over the world like good stories. **Folktales** are good stories that people have liked and told for hundreds of years. Every country has folktales, and India is a country that has many of them. **Tenali Raman** is the name of a character who is in many Indian folktales. Tenali is a young boy who is very poor. He is also very smart and is able to play tricks on people to get what he wants.

Here are some of the words you will read in the story "Tricky Tenali Raman." See if you can tell what each word means by the way it is used in a sentence.

1. The *jester's* tricks and jokes made the king laugh.

   A *jester* is a person who

   a. protects the king.

   b. entertains the king.

   c. helps the king rule the land.

2. The king gathered his *court* into the palace to watch a magic show.

   This *court* means

   a. all the people who live with and work for the king.

   b. a place where laws are passed.

   c. a place where people play tennis.

3. The *boastful* man talked only about himself and what he could do.

   The word *boastful* describes a person who

   a. brags all the time.

   b. can do a lot of things very well.

   c. likes to listen to what other people say.

Scholastic Teaching Resources

Reading the Story

Tenali Raman was a poor country boy, but he was very clever. He wanted to work for the king.

When Tenali Raman arrived at the palace, everyone was watching a magic show. The magician turned scarves into snakes. He pulled gold coins from behind people's ears. With a wave of his hand, the magician made birds appear in the air.

As everyone clapped, the magician bowed and said, "I am the best magician in the world. Is there anyone in the king's court who can perform a trick that I cannot do better?"

When no one answered, the king was embarrassed. No one in his court could perform magic. Suddenly, Tenali Raman shouted, "I know a trick!"

"What trick can a silly boy like you do?" the magician said, laughing.

"I will perform a trick with my eyes closed if you will perform the same trick with your eyes open. Do you think you can do that?" Tenali Raman asked.

"I am a great magician. If you can do a trick with your eyes closed, I am sure I can do it better with my eyes open," replied the magician.

Tenali Raman reached into his pocket and took out a spoon and a bag of hot chili powder. He closed his eyes and dropped the chili powder onto his closed eyelids. He waited a couple of minutes. Then he brushed off the chili powder and opened his eyes. He handed a spoonful of chili powder to the magician. "Now it is your turn, and, remember, your eyes must be open."

"But this is not magic!" the magician shouted. "I cannot do that! The powder will burn my eyes!"

Everyone began to boo and hiss at the boastful magician. He ran from the hall, leaving Tenali Raman to take a big bow. The happy king made Tenali Raman his court jester.

➡ **Thinking About What You Read**

1. Why do you think Tenali Raman wanted to work for the king?

_____

_____

_____

_____

2. The magician can perform very good tricks. Why does he seem not to be a very good person?

_____

_____

_____

_____

3. Tenali Raman was made the king's jester. That means he will have to entertain the king. What do you think Tenali will do to make the king laugh?

_____

_____

_____

_____

Reading Aloud With Expression

The story of Tenali Raman can be rewritten as a play with the following parts: Tenali Raman, the magician, and a narrator.

Practice reading the parts while being sure to make your voice show the different feelings of the characters.

 **Story**

 **Reading Tips**

Narrator: Tenali Raman was a poor country boy, but he was very clever. He wanted to work for the king.

When Tenali Raman arrived at the palace, everyone was watching a magic show. The magician turned scarves into snakes. He pulled gold coins from behind people's ears. With a wave of his hand, the magician made birds appear in the air.

As everyone clapped, the magician bowed.

Magician: "I am the best magician in the world. Is there anyone in the king's court who can perform a trick that I cannot do better?"

It is very important that the narrator read clearly and not too fast. To prepare, use a yellow crayon to mark places where there are commas (,) to remind yourself to pause when reading. Use a red crayon to mark where there are the periods (.) to signal that these are longer pauses.

1. *As the narrator describes the magician's tricks, what emotion should his voice try to show?*

   a. fear

   b. amazement

   c. disbelief

2. *How should the magician's voice sound here?*

   a. proud and boastful

   b. tired and ready to leave

   c. happy and pleased

Scholastic Teaching Resources

 **Story**

 **Reading Tips**

Narrator: When no one answered, the king was embarrassed. No one in his court could perform magic. Suddenly, Tenali Raman shouted.

The narrator should continue to read clearly and to pay attention to punctuation marks. The last line here is what gets the listeners ready for the important part of the story: the trick.

1. *How should the narrator's voice sound?*

   a. quiet

   b. embarrassed like the king

   c. excited

Tenali: "I know a trick!"

2. *What clue tells the reader how to say Tenali's line?*

   _____

   _____

Magician: "What trick can a silly boy like you do?"

Narrator: The magician then laughs.

3. *How should the magician's voice and laugh sound?*

   a. proud and mean

   b. happy

   c. worried

Tenali: "I will perform a trick with my eyes closed if you will perform the same trick with your eyes open. Do you think you can do that?"

4. *Tenali wants to trick the magician, so how does he want the trick to sound?*

   a. very difficult

   b. very easy

Magician: "I am a great magician. If you can do a trick with your eyes closed, I am sure I can do it better with my eyes open."

5. *How should the magician's voice sound when he accepts the challenge?*

   a. proud

   b. happy

   c. worried

Name _____

otags**Tricky Tenali Raman
(Folktale From India)**

Story

Narrator: Tenali Raman reached into his pocket and took out a spoon and a bag of hot chili powder. He closed his eyes and dropped the chili powder onto his closed eyelids. He waited a couple of minutes. Then he brushed off the chili powder and opened his eyes. He handed a spoonful of chili powder to the magician.

Tenali: "Now it is your turn, and, remember, your eyes must be open."

Magician: "But this is not magic! I cannot do that! The powder will burn my eyes!"

Narrator: Everyone began to boo and hiss at the boastful magician. He ran from the hall, leaving Tenali Raman to take a big bow. The happy king made Tenali Raman his court jester.

Reading Tips

The narrator should be sure to pause after each sentence to build suspense for the listeners. This is the part of the story that describes the trick, so it is very important that the listeners understand what happens.

1. *Why do you think Tenali's voice should say "your" just a little louder than the other words when he says this?*

_____

_____

2. *How should the magician's voice sound here?*

   a. excited to try a new trick

   b. surprised and angry that he has been tricked

   c. surprised and happy that he has been tricked

Here the narrator's voice should change. The "boo and hiss" sentence should show everyone was angry. But Tenali's "big bow" and reward are both happy events.

Scholastic Teaching Resources

Scholastic Success With Fluency • Grade 2   47

Page 6
1. Check students' flags. 2. The blue background was for the Alaskan sky and the forget-me-not. 3. The North Star stands for the future state of Alaska, the most northerly state of the Union. 4. The Great Bear shows strength.

Page 7
Answers will vary.

Page 8
1. seals; 2. gently; 3. habitat; 4. steel bars, moats, trenches

Page 11
Answers will vary.

Page 12
g, f, a, b, j, i, c, h, d, e

Page 14
1. F; 2. F; 3. T; 4. T; 5. F; 6. T; Answers will vary.

Page 15
1. Answers will vary. 2. Dinosaur in top left box should be circled. b; 3. 1, 4, 2, 3

Page 16
e, g, d, f, a, c, b

Page 18
1. Sue's ribs had been broken. 2. Sue had many large teeth and sharp claws. Its legs were strong, and it could probably move fast. 3. Sue Hendrickson found the *T. rex* skeleton. 4–5. Answers will vary.

Page 20
1. Germany, Italy, Alps; 2. Hikers; 3. glacier; 4. soles; 5. ancient; 6. tendons

Page 24
Answers will vary.

Page 26
1. angry; 2. scared; 3. amused

Page 27
4. thankful; 5. grateful; 6. proud Answers may vary.

Page 28
"Wolf! Wolf! Help!"

"Where is the wolf?"

"I played a trick on you."

"Why didn't you help me when I called for you?"

"Once you tell a lie, no one will believe you can tell the truth."

Page 30
Answers will vary.

Page 31
Answers will vary.

Page 32

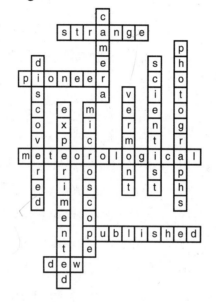

Page 34
1. He spent hours looking at them. He liked to draw them. 2. 3; 3. He liked the beauty of snowflakes. 4. his father, his neighbors; 5. Answers will vary.

Page 35
1. Answers will vary. 2. "White Snow"; 3. Answers will vary.

Page 36
1. motionless; 2. disguise; 3. deliberately; 4. birds, spiders, rodents, reptiles; 5. twig; 6. slender

Page 39
Answers will vary.

Page 41
Answers will vary.

Page 42
1. b; 2. a; 3. a

Page 44
1. Answers will vary. 2. Answers will vary. 3. Answers will vary.

Page 45
1. b; 2. a

Page 46
1. c; 2. exclamation point; 3. a; 4.b; 5. a

Page 47
1. Answers will vary. 2. b

Scholastic Teaching Resources